Collins

Assessment

Spelling Half Termly Tests

Year 5/P6

Clare Dowdall

William Collins' dream of knowledge for all began with the publication of his first book in 1819.
A self-educated mill worker, he not only enriched millions of lives, but also founded a flourishing
publishing house. Today, staying true to this spirit, Collins books are packed with inspiration,
innovation and practical expertise. They place you at the centre of a world of possibility
and give you exactly what you need to explore it.

Collins. Freedom to teach.

Collins
An imprint of HarperCollins*Publishers*
The News Building
1 London Bridge Street
London
SE1 9GF

Browse the complete Collins catalogue at **www.collins.co.uk**

© HarperCollins*Publishers* Limited 2018

10 9 8 7 6 5 4 3 2 1

ISBN 978-0-00-831154-4

British Library Cataloguing in Publication Data. A catalogue record for this publication is available from the British Library.

Author: Clare Dowdall
Publisher: Katie Sergeant
Senior Editor: Mike Appleton
Copyeditor: Tanya Solomons
Proofreader: Catherine Dakin
Cover designer: The Big Mountain Design, Ken Vail Graphic Design
Production controller: Katharine Willard
Printed and bound by CPI Group (UK) Ltd, Croydon, CR0 4YY

Contents

How to use this book

Introduction

Collins Assessment Spelling Half Termly Tests have been designed to give you a consistent whole school approach to teaching and assessing spelling. Each photocopiable book covers the required rules, words and common exception words from the English National Curriculum statutory guidance and Spelling Appendix. For teachers in Scotland, the books can offer guidance and structure that is not provided in the Curriculum for Excellence Experiences and Outcomes or Benchmarks.

Revision of previous years' work is also included, where appropriate, to ensure children are building their skills to become confident and secure spellers. As standalone tests, independent of any teaching and learning scheme, *Collins Assessment Spelling Half Termly Tests* provide a structured way to assess progress in spelling, to identify areas for development, and to provide evidence towards expectations for each year group.

Why spelling matters

Spelling is a key focus of the 2014 English National Curriculum statutory requirements for writing, and the expectations and demands are significant. Out of a possible 70 marks, 20 are awarded for spelling in the Key Stage 2 National Tests, and 20 per cent of the new English Language GCSE 9–1 marks are allocated to spelling, punctuation and grammar. In Year 2, there is an optional Key Stage 1 English grammar, punctuation and spelling test that schools can use to help them make an assessment about children's spelling knowledge, as well as looking at their writing. In Scotland, the P1 literacy, P4 writing and P7 writing Scottish National Standardised Assessments assess spelling at early, first and second levels, respectively.

Focusing on spelling knowledge and skills will also benefit children's wider writing and will have a lasting impact across their education in primary, secondary and beyond. The *Collins Assessment Spelling Half Termly Tests* aim to support teachers to make assessments about children's confidence and use of required spelling rules and strategies, in order to support preparation for these standard assessment points.

How to use this book

The book is divided into two main sections. In the first section, between 30 and 36 weekly word lists are provided (depending on the year group). Each list contains six to ten words per half term. These words can be used for weekly tests and used in the classroom, or sent home with the children. They generally follow the order of the spelling rules as set out in the Spelling Appendix of the National Curriculum and include any words that are specified in the word lists and the non-statutory guidance.

In the second section, 12 half-termly tests are provided, offering two test options per half term: Test A and Test B. These tests offer an equivalent level of challenge and are designed to cover the spelling patterns for that half term's work. The spellings in the half-termly tests are presented in a random order within contextualised sentences. The sentences used are appropriate for the year group in terms of content, grammar and punctuation. The tests are designed to build experience and confidence with this format as well as to test children's spelling knowledge when writing in context.

Each test should take approximately 15 minutes. Guidance is provided for each test, with instructions to read out to the children and a script. The children write the word in the gap in the sentence on their test.

How to use this book

The tests have been written to ensure smooth progression in children's spelling ability within the book and across the rest of the books in series, enabling them to build on their spelling knowledge and show progress.

Marking the tests

The answers are provided in two formats for ease of use: in context and in short form for quick marking.

Recording progress

You can use the pupil-facing record sheets to provide evidence of the areas in which children have performed well and where they need to focus. A spreadsheet is provided in the downloadable version so results can easily be recorded for your classes, and any gaps in understanding can be identified. The spreadsheet can then be used to inform your next teaching and learning steps.

Editable download

All the files are available in Word and PDF format for you to edit if you wish. Go to collins.co.uk/assessment/downloads to find instructions on how to download. The files are password protected and the password clue is included on the website. You will need to use the clue to locate the password in your book.

Year 3/P4 Word lists – Autumn Half Term 1

Word list 1

vicious
precious
conscious
delicious
malicious
suspicious
anxious
gracious
spacious
noxious

Word list 2

ambitious
cautious
fictitious
infectious
nutritious
conscientious
pretentious
repetitious
scrumptious
superstitious

Word list 3

official
special
artificial
financial
commercial
provincial
crucial
facial
official
social

Word list 4

partial
confidential
essential
initial
palatial
potential
residential
sequential
substantial
torrential

Word list 5

observant
expectant
hesitant
tolerant
relevant
reluctant
assistant
brilliant
distant
ignorant

Year 3/P4 Word lists – Autumn Half Term 2

Word list 6

abundance
assistance
dominance
extravagance
fragrance
ignorance
tolerance
reluctance
resistance
tolerance

Word list 7

hesitancy
buoyancy
discrepancy
complacency
infancy
redundancy
truancy
vacancy
stagnancy
pregnancy

Word list 8

innocent
decent
frequent
confident
independent
absent
different
obedient
permanent
violent

Word list 9

obedience
independence
presence
evidence
sentence
sequence
silence
experience
patience
confidence

Word list 10

agency
fluency
decency
urgency
tendency
frequency
emergency
efficiency
deficiency
excellency

Year 3/P4 Word lists – Spring Half Term 1

Word list 1

adorable
applicable
considerable
tolerable
changeable
noticeable
sociable
portable
suitable
valuable

Word list 2

dependable
comfortable
understandable
reasonable
enjoyable
reliable
mixable
capable
readable
drinkable

Word list 3

forcible
legible
edible
visible
incredible
audible
sensible
horrible
flexible
possible

Year 3/P4 Word lists – Spring Half Term 1

Word list 4

reliably
probably
amicably
excitably
miserably
honourably
laughably
agreeably
reasonably
noticeably

Word list 5

possibly
horribly
terribly
visibly
incredibly
sensibly
invisibly
impossibly
responsibly
irresistibly

Year 3/P4 Word lists – Spring Half Term 2

Word list 6

refer
referring
referred
referral
reference
referee
prefer
preferring
preferred
preference

Word list 7

deter
deterring
deterred
deterrence
transfer
transferring
transferred
offer
offering
offered

Word list 8

co-ordinate
re-enter
co-operate
re-use
co-own
re-orientate
co-author
re-align
co-exist
re-attach

Word list 9

deceive
conceive
receive
perceive
ceiling
protein
seize
either
neither
caffeine

Word list 10

conceit
receipt
achieve
believe
brief
piece
grief
fiend
relief
friend

Year 3/P4 Word lists – Summer Half Term 1

Word list 1

ought
bought
thought
nought
brought
fought
rough
tough
enough
cough

Word list 2

though
although
dough
through
thorough
borough
plough
bough
hiccough
trough

Word list 3

doubt
island
lamb
solemn
thistle
knight
debt
tomb
hymn
knock

Word list 4

castle
comb
rhythm
whistle
muscle
knife
knee
limb
thumb
know

Word list 5

advice
advise
device
devise
licence
license
practice
practise
prophecy
prophesy

Year 3/P4 Word lists – Summer Half Term 2

Word list 6

father
farther
guessed
guest
heard
herd
led
lead
morning
mourning

Word list 7

past
passed
proceed
precede
principal
principle
profit
prophet
stationary
stationery

Word list 8

steel
steal
wary
weary
who's
whose
aisle
isle
aloud
allowed

Word list 9

affect
effect
alter
altar
ascent
assent
bridal
bridle
cereal
serial

Word list 10

compliment
complement
descent
dissent
desert
dessert
draft
draught
weigh
way

Year 5/P6 Autumn Half Term 1 Test A

Spelling rules and knowledge

- The words in this test can be used to check knowledge about word endings.
- The sound made by **-cious** or **-tious** at the end of words
- The sound made by **-cial** or **-tial** at the end of words
- Words ending in **-ant**

Guidance for teachers

The test is designed to build experience and confidence with this format, as well as to test children's spelling knowledge.

The test should take approximately 15 minutes.

Children should have a copy of the test and a pencil to use.

Children with specific needs should be given appropriate support.

All children should be encouraged to have a go at spelling each word, using the strategies that they have learnt.

Remind the children to check their answers by asking: *Does it look right? Does it sound right? Does it make sense in the sentence?*

Avoid over-emphasising the spelling of each word as you read it.

> Read each word aloud, saying: *The word is…*
> Next, read the sentence that includes the word.
> Wait for the children to attempt to write the word.
> Re-read the word, saying: *The word is…*

Remind the children to check the word before moving to the next spelling.

At the end of the test, read each sentence again and encourage the children to check back.

Instructions for children

(You may like to read this to the children prior to the test.)

This is a spelling test to check your knowledge of the spelling patterns we have worked on this half term.

You need a pencil.

Please write your name, class and the date at the top of the test.

I will read a word out loud and then say it again in a sentence.

You should write the word in the gap in the sentence on your test.

I will read it again and give you time to check it.

Don't worry if you are not sure about a spelling. Have a go using the strategies we have learnt.

If you make a mistake, cross out the word and try again.

Words tested (20)

precious, cautious, special, confidential, expectant, delicious, infectious, financial, initial, tolerant, anxious, pretentious, crucial, residential, assistant, spacious, scrumptious, official, substantial, distant

Year 5/P6 Autumn Half Term 1 Test A

Spelling script

Spelling 1: The word is **precious**.
The crown was dotted with **precious** sapphires.
The word is **precious**.

Spelling 2: The word is **cautious**.
The **cautious** vet edged nearer to the injured dog.
The word is **cautious**.

Spelling 3: The word is **special**.
For a **special** treat, we stayed up until midnight.
The word is **special**.

Spelling 4: The word is **confidential**.
The **confidential** document was left on the seat of
the train.
The word is **confidential**.

Spelling 5: The word is **expectant**.
The **expectant** children couldn't wait for the day of
the party.
The word is **expectant**.

Spelling 6: The word is **delicious**.
The **delicious** cake attracted the girl's attention.
The word is **delicious**.

Spelling 7: The word is **infectious**.
The deadly virus was terribly **infectious**.
The word is **infectious**.

Spelling 8: The word is **financial**.
The bank manager dealt with the **financial** matters.
The word is **financial**.

Spelling 9: The word is **initial**.
The **initial** letter is used to arrange words in
alphabetical order.
The word is **initial**.

Spelling 10: The word is **tolerant**.
The **tolerant** Labrador allowed the children to pull its
ears.
The word is **tolerant**.

Spelling 11: The word is **anxious**.
She was **anxious** when her brother didn't arrive
home at the usual time.
The word is **anxious**.

Spelling 12: The word is **pretentious**.
The **pretentious** footballer thought he should play
for the Premier League.
The word is **pretentious**.

Spelling 13: The word is **crucial**.
It is **crucial** to wear a seatbelt in a car.
The word is **crucial**.

Spelling 14: The word is **residential**.
The children couldn't wait for their **residential** trip.
The word is **residential**.

Spelling 15: The word is **assistant**.
The shop **assistant** brought me some jeans to try.
The word is **assistant**.

Spelling 16: The word is **spacious**.
The boy's new bedroom was extremely **spacious**.
The word is **spacious**.

Spelling 17: The word is **scrumptious**.
A **scrumptious** feast awaited the guests.
The word is **scrumptious**.

Spelling 18: The word is **official**.
The **official** letter arrived in a brown envelope
marked 'confidential'.
The word is **official**.

Spelling 19: The word is **substantial**.
We spend a **substantial** amount of time outside in
the garden.
The word is **substantial**.

Spelling 20: The word is **distant**.
We could see the sun rising on the **distant** horizon.
The word is **distant**.

Well done! Now I will read the sentences again so you can check your spelling.

Year 5/P6 Autumn Half Term 1 Test A

1. The crown was dotted with _____ sapphires.

2. The _____ vet edged nearer to the injured dog.

3. For a _____ treat, we stayed up until midnight.

4. The _____ document was left on the seat of the train.

5. The _____ children couldn't wait for the day of the party.

6. The _____ cake attracted the girl's attention.

7. The deadly virus was terribly _____.

8. The bank manager dealt with the _____ matters.

9. The _____ letter is used to arrange words in

   alphabetical order.

10. The _____ Labrador allowed the children to pull its ears.

11. She was _____ when her brother didn't arrive home at

    the usual time.

12. The _____ footballer thought he should play for the

    Premier League.

13. It is _____ to wear a seatbelt in a car.

14. The children couldn't wait for their _____ trip.

15. The shop _____ brought me some jeans to try.

16. The boy's new bedroom was extremely _____.

17. A _____ feast awaited the guests.

18. The _____ letter arrived in a brown envelope marked

    'confidential'.

19. We spend a _____ amount of time outside in the garden.

20. We could see the sun rising on the _____ horizon.

Total _____ / 20

Year 5/P6 Autumn Half Term 1 Test B

Spelling rules and knowledge

- The words in this test can be used to check knowledge about word endings.
- The sound made by **-cious** or **-tious** at the end of words
- The sound made by **-cial** or **-tial** at the end of words
- Words ending in **-ant**

Guidance for teachers

The test is designed to build experience and confidence with this format, as well as to test children's spelling knowledge.

The test should take approximately 15 minutes.

Children should have a copy of the test and a pencil to use.

Children with specific needs should be given appropriate support.

All children should be encouraged to have a go at spelling each word, using the strategies that they have learnt.

Remind the children to check their answers by asking: *Does it look right? Does it sound right? Does it make sense in the sentence?*

Avoid over-emphasising the spelling of each word as you read it.

> Read each word aloud, saying: *The word is…*
> Next, read the sentence that includes the word.
> Wait for the children to attempt to write the word.
> Re-read the word, saying: *The word is…*

Remind the children to check the word before moving to the next spelling.

At the end of the test, read each sentence again and encourage the children to check back.

Instructions for children

(You may like to read this to the children prior to the test.)

This is a spelling test to check your knowledge of the spelling patterns we have worked on this half term.

You need a pencil.

Please write your name, class and the date at the top of the test.

I will read a word out loud and then say it again in a sentence.

You should write the word in the gap in the sentence on your test.

I will read it again and give you time to check it.

Don't worry if you are not sure about a spelling. Have a go using the strategies we have learnt.

If you make a mistake, cross out the word and try again.

Words tested (20)

vicious, ambitious, social, partial, observant, conscious, fictitious, artificial, essential, hesitant, malicious, nutritious, commercial, palatial, relevant, suspicious, conscientious, provincial, potential, reluctant

Year 5/P6 Autumn Half Term 1 Test B

Spelling script

Spelling 1: The word is **vicious**.
The **vicious** dog snarled at the quivering thief.
The word is **vicious**.

Spelling 2: The word is **ambitious**.
In an **ambitious** move, the defender slid to the left.
The word is **ambitious**.

Spelling 3: The word is **social**.
The royal wedding was the **social** event of the year.
The word is **social**.

Spelling 4: The word is **partial**.
Ferns prefer to grow in **partial** shade.
The word is **partial**.

Spelling 5: The word is **observant**.
A detective needs to be **observant** to spot clues.
The word is **observant**.

Spelling 6: The word is **conscious**.
Although he banged his head on the pavement, he remained **conscious**.
The word is **conscious**.

Spelling 7: The word is **fictitious**.
Traditional stories like Little Red Riding Hood are **fictitious**, rather than true.
The word is **fictitious**.

Spelling 8: The word is **artificial**.
Robots can use **artificial** intelligence to build cars.
The word is **artificial**.

Spelling 9: The word is **essential**.
It is **essential** to brush your teeth at least twice a day!
The word is **essential**.

Spelling 10: The word is **hesitant**.
She became **hesitant** when she saw the height of the diving board.
The word is **hesitant**.

Spelling 11: The word is **malicious**.
The **malicious** bully sneered at the trembling child.
The word is **malicious**.

Spelling 12: The word is **nutritious**.
Lentils are highly **nutritious**.
The word is **nutritious**.

Spelling 13: The word is **commercial**.
The television **commercial** for fast food was banned from children's TV.
The word is **commercial**.

Spelling 14: The word is **palatial**.
We stayed in luxury at the **palatial** holiday home.
The word is **palatial**.

Spelling 15: The word is **relevant**.
The police officer only wanted to record **relevant** facts about the incident.
The word is **relevant**.

Spelling 16: The word is **suspicious**.
My brother's smiling face made me **suspicious**.
The word is **suspicious**.

Spelling 17: The word is **conscientious**.
A **conscientious** child does their homework without being asked.
The word is **conscientious**.

Spelling 18: The word is **provincial**.
The country town had a **provincial** look about it.
The word is **provincial**.

Spelling 19: The word is **potential**.
Sports people aim to fulfil their **potential**.
The word is **potential**.

Spelling 20: The word is **reluctant**.
He was **reluctant** to spend too much money on new trainers.
The word is **reluctant**.

Well done! Now I will read the sentences again so you can check your spelling.

| Name | Class | Date |

Year 5/P6 Autumn Half Term 1 Test B

1. The _____ dog snarled at the quivering thief.

2. In an _____ move, the defender slid to the left.

3. The royal wedding was the _____ event of the year.

4. Ferns prefer to grow in _____ shade.

5. A detective needs to be _____ to spot clues.

6. Although he banged his head on the pavement, he remained

   _____.

7. Traditional stories like Little Red Riding Hood are _____,

   rather than true.

8. Robots can use _____ intelligence to build cars.

9. It is _____ to brush your teeth at least twice a day!

10. She became _____ when she saw the height of the

    diving board.

11. The _____ bully sneered at the trembling child.

12. Lentils are highly _____.

13. The television _____ for fast food was banned from

children's TV.

14. We stayed in luxury at the _____ holiday home.

15. The police officer only wanted to record _____ facts about

the incident.

16. My brother's smiling face made me _____.

17. A _____ child does their homework without being asked.

18. The country town had a _____ look about it.

19. Sports people aim to fulfil their _____.

20. He was _____ to spend too much money on new trainers.

Total _____ / 20

Year 5/P6 Autumn Half Term 2 Test A

Spelling rules and knowledge

- The words in this test can be used to check knowledge about word endings.
- Words ending in **-ant**, **-ance**, **-ancy**, **-ent**, **-ence**, **-ency**

Guidance for teachers

The test is designed to build experience and confidence with this format, as well as to test children's spelling knowledge.

The test should take approximately 15 minutes.

Children should have a copy of the test and a pencil to use.

Children with specific needs should be given appropriate support.

All children should be encouraged to have a go at spelling each word, using the strategies that they have learnt.

Remind the children to check their answers by asking: *Does it look right? Does it sound right? Does it make sense in the sentence?*

Avoid over-emphasising the spelling of each word as you read it.

> Read each word aloud, saying: *The word is…*
> Next, read the sentence that includes the word.
> Wait for the children to attempt to write the word.
> Re-read the word, saying: *The word is…*

Remind the children to check the word before moving to the next spelling.

At the end of the test, read each sentence again and encourage the children to check back.

Instructions for children

(You may like to read this to the children prior to the test.)

This is a spelling test to check your knowledge of the spelling patterns we have worked on this half term.

You need a pencil.

Please write your name, class and the date at the top of the test.

I will read a word out loud and then say it again in a sentence.

You should write the word in the gap in the sentence on your test.

I will read it again and give you time to check it.

Don't worry if you are not sure about a spelling. Have a go using the strategies we have learnt.

If you make a mistake, cross out the word and try again.

Words tested (20)

assistance, buoyancy, decent, independence, fluency, extravagance, complacency, confident, evidence, urgency, tolerance, truancy, different, silence, emergency, resistance, stagnancy, permanent, patience, deficiency

Year 5/P6 Autumn Half Term 2 Test A

Spelling script

Spelling 1: The word is **assistance**.
Would you like **assistance** with your suitcase?
The word is **assistance**.

Spelling 2: The word is **buoyancy**.
The lifeboat's **buoyancy** was reducing by the second.
The word is **buoyancy**.

Spelling 3: The word is **decent**.
You made a **decent** attempt at tidying up.
The word is **decent**.

Spelling 4: The word is **independence**.
The teenager was desperate to be given more **independence**.
The word is **independence**.

Spelling 5: The word is **fluency**.
We can speak French with **fluency**.
The word is **fluency**.

Spelling 6: The word is **extravagance**.
Sugar on strawberries is a delicious **extravagance**.
The word is **extravagance**.

Spelling 7: The word is **complacency**.
His feeling of **complacency** was destroyed when he lost the game.
The word is **complacency**.

Spelling 8: The word is **confident**.
We are **confident** about our spelling ability!
The word is **confident**.

Spelling 9: The word is **evidence**.
The detective scoured the garden for **evidence** of the crime.
The word is **evidence**.

Spelling 10: The word is **urgency**.
There is absolutely no **urgency** to get out of bed.
The word is **urgency**.

Spelling 11: The word is **tolerance**.
The teacher's **tolerance** was tested by the flickering lights!
The word is **tolerance**.

Spelling 12: The word is **truancy**.
Truancy is a problem in some secondary schools.
The word is **truancy**.

Spelling 13: The word is **different**.
I tried on **different** trainers, but they still pinched my toes.
The word is **different**.

Spelling 14: The word is **silence**.
The **silence** was rather unnerving.
The word is **silence**.

Spelling 15: The word is **emergency**.
In an **emergency**, please leave by the nearest exit.
The word is **emergency**.

Spelling 16: The word is **resistance**.
They showed **resistance** by refusing to wear the new uniform.
The word is **resistance**.

Spelling 17: The word is **stagnancy**.
The **stagnancy** of the water made it undrinkable.
The word is **stagnancy**.

Spelling 18: The word is **permanent**.
The man's tattoo was a **permanent** reminder of his love for his wife.
The word is **permanent**.

Spelling 19: The word is **patience**.
Some say that **patience** is a virtue!
The word is **patience**.

Spelling 20: The word is **deficiency**.
A **deficiency** in vitamins can make you feel unwell.
The word is **deficiency**.

Well done! Now I will read the sentences again so you can check your spelling.

Year 5/P6 Autumn Half Term 2 Test A

1. Would you like _____ with your suitcase?

2. The lifeboat's _____ was reducing by the second.

3. You made a _____ attempt at tidying up.

4. The teenager was desperate to be given more _____.

5. We can speak French with _____.

6. Sugar on strawberries is a delicious _____.

7. His feeling of _____ was destroyed when he lost the game.

8. We are _____ about our spelling ability!

9. The detective scoured the garden for _____ of the crime.

10. There is absolutely no _____ to get out of bed.

11. The teacher's _____ was tested by the flickering lights!

12. _____ is a problem in some secondary schools.

13. I tried on _____ trainers, but they still pinched my toes.

14. The _____ was rather unnerving.

15. In an _____, please leave by the nearest exit.

16. They showed _____ by refusing to wear the new uniform.

17. The _____ of the water made it undrinkable.

18. The man's tattoo was a _____ reminder of his love for

his wife.

19. Some say that _____ is a virtue!

20. A _____ in vitamins can make you feel unwell.

Total _____ / 20

29

Year 5/P6 Autumn Half Term 2 Test B

Spelling rules and knowledge

- The words in this test can be used to check knowledge about word endings.
- Words ending in **-ant**, **-ance**, **-ancy**, **-ent**, **-ence**, **-ency**

Guidance for teachers

The test is designed to build experience and confidence with this format, as well as to test children's spelling knowledge.

The test should take approximately 15 minutes.

Children should have a copy of the test and a pencil to use.

Children with specific needs should be given appropriate support.

All children should be encouraged to have a go at spelling each word, using the strategies that they have learnt.

Remind the children to check their answers by asking: *Does it look right? Does it sound right? Does it make sense in the sentence?*

Avoid over-emphasising the spelling of each word as you read it.

Read each word aloud, saying: *The word is…*
Next, read the sentence that includes the word.
Wait for the children to attempt to write the word.
Re-read the word, saying: *The word is…*

Remind the children to check the word before moving to the next spelling.

At the end of the test, read each sentence again and encourage the children to check back.

Instructions for children

(You may like to read this to the children prior to the test.)

This is a spelling test to check your knowledge of the spelling patterns we have worked on this half term.

You need a pencil.

Please write your name, class and the date at the top of the test.

I will read a word out loud and then say it again in a sentence.

You should write the word in the gap in the sentence on your test.

I will read it again and give you time to check it.

Don't worry if you are not sure about a spelling. Have a go using the strategies we have learnt.

If you make a mistake, cross out the word and try again.

Words tested (20)

abundance, hesitancy, innocent, obedience, agency, dominance, discrepancy, frequent, presence, decency, fragrance, infancy, independent, sentence, tendency, ignorance, redundancy, absent, sequence, frequency

Year 5/P6 Autumn Half Term 2 Test B

Spelling script

Spelling 1: The word is **abundance**.
There was an **abundance** of apples in the orchard.
The word is **abundance**.

Spelling 2: The word is **hesitancy**.
There was **hesitancy** in her voice as she sang.
The word is **hesitancy**.

Spelling 3: The word is **innocent**.
The **innocent** girl was wrongly accused of stealing.
The word is **innocent**.

Spelling 4: The word is **obedience**.
Our puppy goes to **obedience** classes.
The word is **obedience**.

Spelling 5: The word is **agency**.
The dress **agency** sells ball gowns and tiaras.
The word is **agency**.

Spelling 6: The word is **dominance**.
His **dominance** on the field was obvious when he
scored a try.
The word is **dominance**.

Spelling 7: The word is **discrepancy**.
There was a **discrepancy** between what he earned
and what he was paid.
The word is **discrepancy**.

Spelling 8: The word is **frequent**.
On **frequent** occasions she got distracted.
The word is **frequent**.

Spelling 9: The word is **presence**.
The storyteller's **presence** filled them with
suspense.
The word is **presence**.

Spelling 10: The word is **decency**.
The girl's **decency** showed when she donated her
gift to the charity.
The word is **decency**.

Spelling 11: The word is **fragrance**.
Mum loves to wear French **fragrance**.
The word is **fragrance**.

Spelling 12: The word is **infancy**.
In early **infancy**, some children go to pre-school.
The word is **infancy**.

Spelling 13: The word is **independent**.
I feel **independent** when I ride my bike.
The word is **independent**.

Spelling 14: The word is **sentence**.
The judge gave a harsh **sentence** to the car thief.
The word is **sentence**.

Spelling 15: The word is **tendency**.
She had a **tendency** to speak without thinking.
The word is **tendency**.

Spelling 16: The word is **ignorance**.
His **ignorance** of the school rules led him into
trouble.
The word is **ignorance**.

Spelling 17: The word is **redundancy**.
The man used his **redundancy** pay to buy a new
caravan.
The word is **redundancy**.

Spelling 18: The word is **absent**.
We try not to be **absent** from school on too many
occasions.
The word is **absent**.

Spelling 19: The word is **sequence**.
A strange **sequence** of events led to his
disappearance.
The word is **sequence**.

Spelling 20: The word is **frequency**.
I try to eat vegetables with increased **frequency**.
The word is **frequency**.

Well done! Now I will read the sentences again so you can check your spelling.

Year 5/P6 Autumn Half Term 2 Test B

1.   There was an _____ of apples in the orchard.

2.   There was _____ in her voice as she sang.

3.   The _____ girl was wrongly accused of stealing.

4.   Our puppy goes to _____ classes.

5.   The dress _____ sells ball gowns and tiaras.

6.   His _____ on the field was obvious when he scored a try.

7.   There was a _____ between what he earned and what

      he was paid.

8.   On _____ occasions she got distracted.

9.   The storyteller's _____ filled them with suspense.

10.   The girl's _____ showed when she donated her gift to

      the charity.

11. Mum loves to wear French _____.

12. In early _____, some children go to pre-school.

13. I feel _____ when I ride my bike.

14. The judge gave a harsh _____ to the car thief.

15. She had a _____ to speak without thinking.

16. His _____ of the school rules led him into trouble.

17. The man used his _____ pay to buy a new caravan.

18. We try not to be _____ from school on too many occasions.

19. A strange _____ of events led to his disappearance.

20. I try to eat green vegetables with increased _____.

Total _____ **/ 20**

Year 5/P6 Spring Half Term 1 Test A

Spelling rules and knowledge

- The words in this test can be used to check knowledge about word endings.
- Words ending in **-able**, **-ible**, **-ably**, **-ibly**

Guidance for teachers

The test is designed to build experience and confidence with this format, as well as to test children's spelling knowledge.

The test should take approximately 15 minutes.

Children should have a copy of the test and a pencil to use.

Children with specific needs should be given appropriate support.

All children should be encouraged to have a go at spelling each word, using the strategies that they have learnt.

Remind the children to check their answers by asking: *Does it look right? Does it sound right? Does it make sense in the sentence?*

Avoid over-emphasising the spelling of each word as you read it.

> Read each word aloud, saying: *The word is…*
> Next, read the sentence that includes the word.
> Wait for the children to attempt to write the word.
> Re-read the word, saying: *The word is…*

Remind the children to check the word before moving to the next spelling.

At the end of the test, read each sentence again and encourage the children to check back.

Instructions for children

(You may like to read this to the children prior to the test.)

This is a spelling test to check your knowledge of the spelling patterns we have worked on this half term.

You need a pencil.

Please write your name, class and the date at the top of the test.

I will read a word out loud and then say it again in a sentence.

You should write the word in the gap in the sentence on your test.

I will read it again and give you time to check it.

Don't worry if you are not sure about a spelling. Have a go using the strategies we have learnt.

If you make a mistake, cross out the word and try again.

Words tested (20)

considerable, understandable, edible, amicably, terribly, changeable, enjoyable, incredible, miserably, impossibly, noticeable, reliable, audible, honourably, sensibly, valuable, drinkable, possible, noticeably, irresistibly

Year 5/P6 Spring Half Term 1 Test A

Spelling script

Spelling 1: The word is **considerable**.
There was **considerable** tension in the exam room.
The word is **considerable**.

Spelling 2: The word is **understandable**.
Her excitement about the new bike was
understandable.
The word is **understandable**.

Spelling 3: The word is **edible**.
The burnt toast was barely **edible**.
The word is **edible**.

Spelling 4: The word is **amicably**.
Despite the argument, they left the playground
amicably.
The word is **amicably**.

Spelling 5: The word is **terribly**.
It was **terribly** hot in the greenhouse.
The word is **terribly**.

Spelling 6: The word is **changeable**.
The weather in the morning is forecast to be
changeable.
The word is **changeable**.

Spelling 7: The word is **enjoyable**.
The trip to the cinema was really **enjoyable**.
The word is **enjoyable**.

Spelling 8: The word is **incredible**.
His **incredible** memory allowed him to learn whole
poems with ease.
The word is **incredible**.

Spelling 9: The word is **miserably**.
He failed **miserably** when he tried to cheer her up.
The word is **miserably**.

Spelling 10: The word is **impossibly**.
The test seemed **impossibly** difficult.
The word is **impossibly**.

Spelling 11: The word is **noticeable**.
The scar on his cheek was barely **noticeable**.
The word is **noticeable**.

Spelling 12: The word is **reliable**.
He was a **reliable** helper who never failed to turn up.
The word is **reliable**.

Spelling 13: The word is **audible**.
The music from his headphones was **audible** from
the other side of the room.
The word is **audible**.

Spelling 14: The word is **honourably**.
She behaved **honourably**, despite her desire to
make a fuss.
The word is **honourably**.

Spelling 15: The word is **sensibly**.
Sensibly, the children lined up at the door.
The word is **sensibly**.

Spelling 16: The word is **valuable**.
The boy learnt a **valuable** lesson when he listened
to the story.
The word is **valuable**.

Spelling 17: The word is **drinkable**.
The tap water in the hostel was **drinkable**.
The word is **drinkable**.

Spelling 18: The word is **possible**.
Is it **possible** to ride a bike safely with no hands?
The word is **possible**.

Spelling 19: The word is **noticeably**.
The temperature in the room became **noticeably**
cooler.
The word is **noticeably**.

Spelling 20: The word is **irresistibly**.
Some bears are **irresistibly** attracted to honey.
The word is **irresistibly**.

Well done! Now I will read the sentences again so you can check your spelling.

Year 5/P6 Spring Half Term 1 Test A

1.   There was _____ tension in the exam room.

2.   Her excitement about the new bike was _____.

3.   The burnt toast was barely _____.

4.   Despite the argument, they left the playground _____.

5.   It was _____ hot in the greenhouse.

6.   The weather in the morning is forecast to be _____.

7.   The trip to the cinema was really _____.

8.   His _____ memory allowed him to learn whole poems

     with ease.

9.   He failed _____ when he tried to cheer her up.

10. The test seemed _____ difficult.

11. The scar on his cheek was barely _____.

12. He was a _____ helper who never failed to turn up.

13. The music from his headphones was _____ from the other

side of the room.

14. She behaved _____, despite her desire to make a fuss.

15. _____, the children lined up at the door.

16. The boy learnt a _____ lesson when he listened to the story.

17. The tap water in the hostel was _____.

18. Is it _____ to ride a bike safely with no hands?

19. The temperature in the room became _____ cooler.

20. Some bears are _____ attracted to honey.

Total _____ / 20

Year 5/P6 Spring Half Term 1 Test B

Spelling rules and knowledge

- The words in this test can be used to check knowledge about word endings.
- Words ending in **-able**, **-ible**, **-ably**, **-ibly**

Guidance for teachers

The test is designed to build experience and confidence with this format, as well as to test children's spelling knowledge.

The test should take approximately 15 minutes.

Children should have a copy of the test and a pencil to use.

Children with specific needs should be given appropriate support.

All children should be encouraged to have a go at spelling each word, using the strategies that they have learnt.

Remind the children to check their answers by asking: *Does it look right? Does it sound right? Does it make sense in the sentence?*

Avoid over-emphasising the spelling of each word as you read it.

Read each word aloud, saying: *The word is…*
Next, read the sentence that includes the word.
Wait for the children to attempt to write the word.
Re-read the word, saying: *The word is…*

Remind the children to check the word before moving to the next spelling.

At the end of the test, read each sentence again and encourage the children to check back.

Instructions for children

(You may like to read this to the children prior to the test.)

This is a spelling test to check your knowledge of the spelling patterns we have worked on this half term.

You need a pencil.

Please write your name, class and the date at the top of the test.

I will read a word out loud and then say it again in a sentence.

You should write the word in the gap in the sentence on your test.

I will read it again and give you time to check it.

Don't worry if you are not sure about a spelling. Have a go using the strategies we have learnt.

If you make a mistake, cross out the word and try again.

Words tested (20)

adorable, dependable, forcible, reliably, possibly, tolerable, reasonable, visible, excitably, visibly, sociable, mixable, sensible, laughably, invisibly, suitable, readable, flexible, reasonably, responsibly

Year 5/P6 Spring Half Term 1 Test B

Spelling script

Spelling 1: The word is **adorable**.
The **adorable** kitten attracted the girls' attention.
The word is **adorable**.

Spelling 2: The word is **dependable**.
She was the most **dependable** volunteer and
always wanted to help.
The word is **dependable**.

Spelling 3: The word is **forcible**.
The guards made a **forcible** entry into the prisoner's
cell.
The word is **forcible**.

Spelling 4: The word is **reliably**.
She turned up **reliably**, time after time.
The word is **reliably**.

Spelling 5: The word is **possibly**.
It was **possibly** the wettest day of the whole
summer.
The word is **possibly**.

Spelling 6: The word is **tolerable**.
His prickly heat rash was barely **tolerable**.
The word is **tolerable**.

Spelling 7: The word is **reasonable**.
The new computer game was a **reasonable** price.
The word is **reasonable**.

Spelling 8: The word is **visible**.
The skier was barely **visible** on the snowy hillside.
The word is **visible**.

Spelling 9: The word is **excitably**.
The little children queued **excitably** for the bouncy
castle.
The word is **excitably**.

Spelling 10: The word is **visibly**.
She was **visibly** upset by the sad story.
The word is **visibly**.

Spelling 11: The word is **sociable**.
The **sociable** bus driver greeted all his passengers
with "Hello!"
The word is **sociable**.

Spelling 12: The word is **mixable**.
The butter was so cold that it was barely **mixable**.
The word is **mixable**.

Spelling 13: The word is **sensible**.
You have just made a very **sensible** suggestion.
The word is **sensible**.

Spelling 14: The word is **laughably**.
She was **laughably** late for the interview.
The word is **laughably**.

Spelling 15: The word is **invisibly**.
She crept **invisibly** into the back of the cave and hid
from the hunter.
The word is **invisibly**.

Spelling 16: The word is **suitable**.
Your footwear isn't **suitable** for the muddy park.
The word is **suitable**.

Spelling 17: The word is **readable**.
The writing on the treasure map was barely
readable.
The word is **readable**.

Spelling 18: The word is **flexible**.
The gymnast's body was strong and **flexible**.
The word is **flexible**.

Spelling 19: The word is **reasonably**.
I am **reasonably** confident that we will win the cup.
The word is **reasonably**.

Spelling 20: The word is **responsibly**.
He walked the dog **responsibly** along the busy
road.
The word is **responsibly**.

Well done! Now I will read the sentences again so you can check your spelling.

Name	Class	Date

Year 5/P6 Spring Half Term 1 Test B

1. The _____ kitten attracted the girls' attention.

2. She was the most _____ volunteer and always wanted to help.

3. The guards made a _____ entry into the prisoner's cell.

4. She turned up _____, time after time.

5. It was _____ the wettest day of the whole summer.

6. His prickly heat rash was barely _____.

7. The new computer game was a _____ price.

8. The skier was barely _____ on the snowy hillside.

9. The little children queued _____ for the bouncy castle.

10. She was _____ upset by the sad story.

11. The _____ bus driver greeted all his passengers with "Hello!"

12. The butter was so cold that it was barely _____.

13. You have just made a very _____ suggestion.

14. She was _____ late for the interview.

15. She crept _____ into the back of the cave and hid from

    the hunter.

16. Your footwear isn't _____ for the muddy park.

17. The writing on the treasure map was barely _____.

18. The gymnast's body was strong and _____.

19. I am _____ confident that we will win the cup.

20. He walked the dog _____ along the busy road.

Total _____ / 20

Year 5/P6 Spring Half Term 2 Test A

Spelling rules and knowledge

- Adding suffixes beginning with vowel letters to words ending in **-fer**
- The sound made by **ei**, sometimes after **c**
- Use of the hyphen

Guidance for teachers

The test is designed to build experience and confidence with this format, as well as to test children's spelling knowledge.

The test should take approximately 15 minutes.

Children should have a copy of the test and a pencil to use.

Children with specific needs should be given appropriate support.

All children should be encouraged to have a go at spelling each word, using the strategies that they have learnt.

Remind the children to check their answers by asking: *Does it look right? Does it sound right? Does it make sense in the sentence?*

Avoid over-emphasising the spelling of each word as you read it.

> Read each word aloud, saying: *The word is…*
> Next, read the sentence that includes the word.
> Wait for the children to attempt to write the word.
> Re-read the word, saying: *The word is…*

Remind the children to check the word before moving to the next spelling.

At the end of the test, read each sentence again and encourage the children to check back.

Instructions for children

(You may like to read this to the children prior to the test.)

This is a spelling test to check your knowledge of the spelling patterns we have worked on this half term.

You need a pencil.

Please write your name, class and the date at the top of the test.

I will read a word out loud and then say it again in a sentence.

You should write the word in the gap in the sentence on your test.

I will read it again and give you time to check it.

Don't worry if you are not sure about a spelling. Have a go using the strategies we have learnt.

If you make a mistake, cross out the word and try again.

Words tested (20)

referred, deterred, co-operate, receive, achieve, reference, transfer, co-own, ceiling, brief, referee, transferring, re-orientate, protein, piece, preference, offered, re-attach, caffeine, friend

Year 5/P6 Spring Half Term 2 Test A

Spelling script

Spelling 1: The word is **referred**.
She **referred** to the dictionary to check the spelling.
The word is **referred**.

Spelling 2: The word is **deterred**.
They could not be **deterred** from eating the cake!
The word is **deterred**.

Spelling 3: The word is **co-operate**.
When you **co-operate**, you can achieve more than
on your own.
The word is **co-operate**.

Spelling 4: The word is **receive**.
He was ready to **receive** his medal from the judge.
The word is **receive**.

Spelling 5: The word is **achieve**.
The teacher wanted his children to **achieve** the best
results possible.
The word is **achieve**.

Spelling 6: The word is **reference**.
The **reference** book fell open at the picture of the
huge tarantula.
The word is **reference**.

Spelling 7: The word is **transfer**.
We can **transfer** the co-ordinates to the map.
The word is **transfer**.

Spelling 8: The word is **co-own**.
The girls were prepared to **co-own** the pony.
The word is **co-own**.

Spelling 9: The word is **ceiling**.
The **ceiling** needed painting following the fizzy drink
explosion.
The word is **ceiling**.

Spelling 10: The word is **brief**.
You can make a **brief** visit to the shop today.
The word is **brief**.

Spelling 11: The word is **referee**.
The **referee** blew his whistle to end the game.
The word is **referee**.

Spelling 12: The word is **transferring**.
We struggled when **transferring** the goldfish from
the jar to the fish tank.
The word is **transferring**.

Spelling 13: The word is **re-orientate**.
It was hard to **re-orientate** ourselves when we came
out into the light.
The word is **re-orientate**.

Spelling 14: The word is **protein**.
Meat and cheese give us **protein** in our diet.
The word is **protein**.

Spelling 15: The word is **piece**.
Who would like a **piece** of fruit cake?
The word is **piece**.

Spelling 16: The word is **preference**.
Please tick the menu to show your **preference**.
The word is **preference**.

Spelling 17: The word is **offered**.
She kindly **offered** me a lift when it was raining.
The word is **offered**.

Spelling 18: The word is **re-attach**.
We tried, unsuccessfully, to **re-attach** the broken
handle.
The word is **re-attach**.

Spelling 19: The word is **caffeine**.
Some fizzy drinks contain **caffeine** and food
colourings.
The word is **caffeine**.

Spelling 20: The word is **friend**.
His best **friend** was invited for a sleepover.
The word is **friend**.

Well done! Now I will read the sentences again so you can check your spelling.

Year 5/P6 Spring Half Term 2 Test A

1. She _____ to the dictionary to check the spelling.

2. They could not be _____ from eating the cake!

3. When you _____, you can achieve more than on your own.

4. He was ready to _____ his medal from the judge.

5. The teacher wanted his children to _____ the best results possible.

6. The _____ book fell open at the picture of the huge tarantula.

7. We can _____ the co-ordinates to the map.

8. The girls were prepared to _____ the pony.

9. The _____ needed painting following the fizzy drink explosion.

10. You can make a _____ visit to the shop today.

11. The _____ blew his whistle to end the game.

12. We struggled when _____ the goldfish from the jar to

    the fish tank.

13. It was hard to _____ ourselves when we came out into

    the light.

14. Meat and cheese give us _____ in our diet.

15. Who would like a _____ of fruit cake?

16. Please tick the menu to show your _____.

17. She kindly _____ me a lift when it was raining.

18. We tried, unsuccessfully, to _____ the broken handle.

19. Some fizzy drinks contain _____ and food colourings.

20. His best _____ was invited for a sleepover.

Total _____ / 20

Year 5/P6 Spring Half Term 2 Test B

Spelling rules and knowledge

- Adding suffixes beginning with vowel letters to words ending in **-fer**
- The sound made by **ei**, sometimes after **c**
- Use of the hyphen

Guidance for teachers

The test is designed to build experience and confidence with this format, as well as to test children's spelling knowledge.

The test should take approximately 15 minutes.

Children should have a copy of the test and a pencil to use.

Children with specific needs should be given appropriate support.

All children should be encouraged to have a go at spelling each word, using the strategies that they have learnt.

Remind the children to check their answers by asking: *Does it look right? Does it sound right? Does it make sense in the sentence?*

Avoid over-emphasising the spelling of each word as you read it.

Read each word aloud, saying: *The word is…*

Next, read the sentence that includes the word.

Wait for the children to attempt to write the word.

Re-read the word, saying: *The word is…*

Remind the children to check the word before moving to the next spelling.

At the end of the test, read each sentence again and encourage the children to check back.

Instructions for children

(You may like to read this to the children prior to the test.)

This is a spelling test to check your knowledge of the spelling patterns we have worked on this half term.

You need a pencil.

Please write your name, class and the date at the top of the test.

I will read a word out loud and then say it again in a sentence.

You should write the word in the gap in the sentence on your test.

I will read it again and give you time to check it.

Don't worry if you are not sure about a spelling. Have a go using the strategies we have learnt.

If you make a mistake, cross out the word and try again.

Words tested (20)

referring, deterring, co-ordinate, deceive, conceit, referral, deterrence, re-use, perceive, believe, preferring, transferred, co-author, seize, grief, preferred, offering, co-exist, neither, relief

Year 5/P6 Spring Half Term 2 Test B

Spelling script

Spelling 1: The word is **referring**.
He kept **referring** to his beloved pet chameleon.
The word is **referring**.

Spelling 2: The word is **deterring**.
There was no **deterring** them from their quest to reach the fifth level of the game.
The word is **deterring**.

Spelling 3: The word is **co-ordinate**.
We needed to **co-ordinate** our plans for the trip.
The word is **co-ordinate**.

Spelling 4: The word is **deceive**.
The boy's story didn't **deceive** his father.
The word is **deceive**.

Spelling 5: The word is **conceit**.
She was puffed up with **conceit** at her cleverness.
The word is **conceit**.

Spelling 6: The word is **referral**.
The doctor made a **referral** for the boy to see the orthopaedic surgeon about his broken wrist.
The word is **referral**.

Spelling 7: The word is **deterrence**.
Many believe that powerful weapons are no **deterrence** in a war situation.
The word is **deterrence**.

Spelling 8: The word is **re-use**.
We **re-use** our water bottles to help the environment.
The word is **re-use**.

Spelling 9: The word is **perceive**.
Mum can **perceive** how I feel by looking at my face.
The word is **perceive**.

Spelling 10: The word is **believe**.
If you **believe** in yourself, you can succeed.
The word is **believe**.

Spelling 11: The word is **preferring**.
We ran into the sea, **preferring** not to linger on the sharp pebbles.
The word is **preferring**.

Spelling 12: The word is **transferred**.
The international football player was **transferred** by his club to another team.
The word is **transferred**.

Spelling 13: The word is **co-author**.
Two or more children can **co-author** a story.
The word is **co-author**.

Spelling 14: The word is **seize**.
We attempted to **seize** the escaping hamster.
The word is **seize**.

Spelling 15: The word is **grief**.
The child's tears of **grief** were wiped away by his father.
The word is **grief**.

Spelling 16: The word is **preferred**.
She **preferred** salted caramel to vanilla ice cream.
The word is **preferred**.

Spelling 17: The word is **offering**.
Thank you for **offering** to carry my heavy bag.
The word is **offering**.

Spelling 18: The word is **co-exist**.
The enemies could not **co-exist** in the same room.
The word is **co-exist**.

Spelling 19: The word is **neither**.
He had **neither** the will nor the desire to join in with the game of volleyball.
The word is **neither**.

Spelling 20: The word is **relief**.
It was such a **relief** to finish the marathon!
The word is **relief**.

Well done! Now I will read the sentences again so you can check your spelling.

Year 5/P6 Spring Half Term 2 Test B

1. He kept _____ to his beloved pet chameleon.

2. There was no _____ them from their quest to reach the

    fifth level of the game.

3. We needed to _____ our plans for the trip.

4. The boy's story didn't _____ his father.

5. She was puffed up with _____ at her cleverness.

6. The doctor made a _____ for the boy to see the orthopaedic

    surgeon about his broken wrist.

7. Many believe that powerful weapons are no _____ in a war

    situation.

8. We _____ our water bottles to help the environment.

9. Mum can _____ how I feel by looking at my face.

10. If you _____ in yourself, you can succeed.

11. We ran into the sea, _____ not to linger on the sharp

pebbles.

12. The international football player was _____ by his club to

another team.

13. Two or more children can _____ a story.

14. We attempted to _____ the escaping hamster.

15. The child's tears of _____ were wiped away by his father.

16. She _____ salted caramel to vanilla ice cream.

17. Thank you for _____ to carry my heavy bag.

18. The enemies could not _____ in the same room.

19. He had _____ the will nor the desire to join in with the game

of volleyball.

20. It was such a _____ to finish the marathon!

Total _____ / 20

Year 5/P6 Summer Half Term 1 Test A

Spelling rules and knowledge

- Words containing the letter string **-ough**
- Words with silent letters
- Homophones and other easily confused words

Guidance for teachers

The test is designed to build experience and confidence with this format, as well as to test children's spelling knowledge.

The test should take approximately 15 minutes.

Children should have a copy of the test and a pencil to use.

Children with specific needs should be given appropriate support.

All children should be encouraged to have a go at spelling each word, using the strategies that they have learnt.

Remind the children to check their answers by asking: *Does it look right? Does it sound right? Does it make sense in the sentence?*

Avoid over-emphasising the spelling of each word as you read it.

> Read each word aloud, saying: *The word is…*
> Next, read the sentence that includes the word.
> Wait for the children to attempt to write the word.
> Re-read the word, saying: *The word is…*

Remind the children to check the word before moving to the next spelling.

At the end of the test, read each sentence again and encourage the children to check back.

Instructions for children

(You may like to read this to the children prior to the test.)

This is a spelling test to check your knowledge of the spelling patterns we have worked on this half term.

You need a pencil.

Please write your name, class and the date at the top of the test.

I will read a word out loud and then say it again in a sentence.

You should write the word in the gap in the sentence on your test.

I will read it again and give you time to check it.

Don't worry if you are not sure about a spelling. Have a go using the strategies we have learnt.

If you make a mistake, cross out the word and try again.

Words tested (20)

bought, although, island, comb, advise, brought, thorough, thistle, muscle, licence, rough, plough, debt, knee, practice, enough, borough, hymn, thumb, devise

Year 5/P6 Summer Half Term 1 Test A

Spelling script

Spelling 1: The word is **bought**.
We **bought** a new game for our console.
The word is **bought**.

Spelling 2: The word is **although**.
Although it was really late, we pleaded to stay up
until the end of the film.
The word is **although**.

Spelling 3: The word is **island**.
Can you swim to the **island** and back before tea?
The word is **island**.

Spelling 4: The word is **comb**.
She tried to **comb** her tangled hair without crying.
The word is **comb**.

Spelling 5: The word is **advise**.
He tried to **advise** his son on which skills he should
develop on the pitch.
The word is **advise**.

Spelling 6: The word is **brought**.
We **brought** our PE kit to school for sports day.
The word is **brought**.

Spelling 7: The word is **thorough**.
The child made a **thorough** search of the
playground.
The word is **thorough**.

Spelling 8: The word is **thistle**.
The **thistle** became tangled in the dog's fur.
The word is **thistle**.

Spelling 9: The word is **muscle**.
Every **muscle** in their bodies ached after the hike.
The word is **muscle**.

Spelling 10: The word is **licence**.
Dad needed to get a fishing **licence** for our day at
the river.
The word is **licence**.

Spelling 11: The word is **rough**.
He put special tyres on his mountain bike to cope
with the **rough** ground.
The word is **rough**.

Spelling 12: The word is **plough**.
The farmer had to **plough** the field before planting.
The word is **plough**.

Spelling 13: The word is **debt**.
She repaid her **debt**, one pound at a time.
The word is **debt**.

Spelling 14: The word is **knee**.
My **knee** was bruised when I fell off my skateboard.
The word is **knee**.

Spelling 15: The word is **practice**.
The **practice** was open for patients every morning at
8:00 a.m.
The word is **practice**.

Spelling 16: The word is **enough**.
You need to drink **enough** water to keep you well-
hydrated on a hot day.
The word is **enough**.

Spelling 17: The word is **borough**.
The **borough** council planted more trees.
The word is **borough**.

Spelling 18: The word is **hymn**.
Sometimes a **hymn** is sung at a church wedding.
The word is **hymn**.

Spelling 19: The word is **thumb**.
The little boy sucked his **thumb** for comfort.
The word is **thumb**.

Spelling 20: The word is **devise**.
The children tried to **devise** a plan to avoid doing
their homework.
The word is **devise**.

Well done! Now I will read the sentences again so you can check your spelling.

Year 5/P6 Summer Half Term 1 Test A

1. We _____ a new game for our console.

2. _____ it was really late, we pleaded to stay up until the end of the film.

3. Can you swim to the _____ and back before tea?

4. She tried to _____ her tangled hair without crying.

5. He tried to _____ his son on which skills he should develop on the pitch.

6. We _____ our PE kit to school for sports day.

7. The child made a _____ search of the playground.

8. The _____ became tangled in the dog's fur.

9. Every _____ in their bodies ached after the hike.

10. Dad needed to get a fishing _____ for our day at the river.

11. He put special tyres on his mountain bike to cope with the

    _____ ground.

12. The farmer had to _____ the field before planting.

13. She repaid her _____, one pound at a time.

14. My _____ was bruised when I fell off my skateboard.

15. The _____ was open for patients every morning at 8:00 a.m.

16. You need to drink _____ water to keep you well-hydrated on

    a hot day.

17. The _____ council planted more trees.

18. Sometimes a _____ is sung at a church wedding.

19. The little boy sucked his _____ for comfort.

20. The children tried to _____ a plan to avoid doing their

    homework.

Total _____ / 20

Year 5/P6 Summer Half Term 1 Test B

Spelling rules and knowledge

- Words containing the letter string **-ough**
- Words with silent letters
- Homophones and other easily confused words

Guidance for teachers

The test is designed to build experience and confidence with this format, as well as to test children's spelling knowledge.

The test should take approximately 15 minutes.

Children should have a copy of the test and a pencil to use.

Children with specific needs should be given appropriate support.

All children should be encouraged to have a go at spelling each word, using the strategies that they have learnt.

Remind the children to check their answers by asking: *Does it look right? Does it sound right? Does it make sense in the sentence?*

Avoid over-emphasising the spelling of each word as you read it.

> Read each word aloud, saying: *The word is…*
> Next, read the sentence that includes the word.
> Wait for the children to attempt to write the word.
> Re-read the word, saying: *The word is…*

Remind the children to check the word before moving to the next spelling.

At the end of the test, read each sentence again and encourage the children to check back.

Instructions for children

(You may like to read this to the children prior to the test.)

This is a spelling test to check your knowledge of the spelling patterns we have worked on this half term.

You need a pencil.

Please write your name, class and the date at the top of the test.

I will read a word out loud and then say it again in a sentence.

You should write the word in the gap in the sentence on your test.

I will read it again and give you time to check it.

Don't worry if you are not sure about a spelling. Have a go using the strategies we have learnt.

If you make a mistake, cross out the word and try again.

Words tested (20)

thought, dough, lamb, rhythm, device, ought, though, doubt, castle, advice, tough, bough, tomb, limb, practise, cough, trough, knock, know, license

Year 5/P6 Summer Half Term 1 Test B

Spelling script

Spelling 1: The word is **thought**.
We **thought** that the referee's decision was fair.
The word is **thought**.

Spelling 2: The word is **dough**.
We make bread **dough** using wholemeal flour.
The word is **dough**.

Spelling 3: The word is **lamb**.
The **lamb** was given a blue mark to identify it.
The word is **lamb**.

Spelling 4: The word is **rhythm**.
To be a good drummer requires a strong sense of **rhythm**.
The word is **rhythm**.

Spelling 5: The word is **device**.
Please turn off your mobile **device**!
The word is **device**.

Spelling 6: The word is **ought**.
You **ought** to be in bed by now.
The word is **ought**.

Spelling 7: The word is **though**.
Even **though** it was raining, the children wanted to bounce on the trampoline.
The word is **though**.

Spelling 8: The word is **doubt**.
She did not **doubt** his story about the lost homework.
The word is **doubt**.

Spelling 9: The word is **castle**.
The **castle** was stormed by armoured soldiers.
The word is **castle**.

Spelling 10: The word is **advice**.
Mum sought **advice** from a gardening expert before choosing new plants.
The word is **advice**.

Spelling 11: The word is **tough**.
The marathon runners had to be **tough** to finish the race.
The word is **tough**.

Spelling 12: The word is **bough**.
The children nestled in the **bough** of the tree.
The word is **bough**.

Spelling 13: The word is **tomb**.
The old stone **tomb** was deathly cold and covered in moss.
The word is **tomb**.

Spelling 14: The word is **limb**.
The vet wrapped a bandage around the dog's damaged **limb**.
The word is **limb**.

Spelling 15: The word is **practise**.
You need to **practise** the piano every day.
The word is **practise**.

Spelling 16: The word is **cough**.
His hacking **cough** kept him awake at night.
The word is **cough**.

Spelling 17: The word is **trough**.
The farmer filled the **trough** with hay for the ponies.
The word is **trough**.

Spelling 18: The word is **knock**.
We dared him to **knock** on the solid oak door.
The word is **knock**.

Spelling 19: The word is **know**.
Do you **know** how to mend a puncture?
The word is **know**.

Spelling 20: The word is **license**.
The council agreed to **license** the building for the party.
The word is **license**.

Well done! Now I will read the sentences again so you can check your spelling.

Year 5/P6 Summer Half Term 1 Test B

1.   We _____ that the referee's decision was fair.

2.   We make bread _____ using wholemeal flour.

3.   The _____ was given a blue mark to identify it.

4.   To be a good drummer requires a strong sense of _____.

5.   Please turn off your mobile _____!

6.   You _____ to be in bed by now.

7.   Even _____ it was raining, the children wanted to bounce on the trampoline.

8.   She did not _____ his story about the lost homework.

9.   The _____ was stormed by armoured soldiers.

10. Mum sought _____ from a gardening expert before choosing new plants.

11.   The marathon runners had to be _____ to finish the race.

12.   The children nestled in the _____ of the tree.

13.   The old stone _____ was deathly cold and covered in moss.

14.   The vet wrapped a bandage around the dog's damaged _____.

15.   You need to _____ the piano every day.

16.   His hacking _____ kept him awake at night.

17.   The farmer filled the _____ with hay for the ponies.

18.   We dared him to _____ on the solid oak door.

19.   Do you _____ how to mend a puncture?

20.   The council agreed to _____ the building for the party.

Total _____ / 20

Year 5/P6 Summer Half Term 2 Test A

Spelling rules and knowledge

- Homophones and other easily confused words

Guidance for teachers

The test is designed to build experience and confidence with this format, as well as to test children's spelling knowledge.
The test should take approximately 15 minutes.
Children should have a copy of the test and a pencil to use.
Children with specific needs should be given appropriate support.
All children should be encouraged to have a go at spelling each word, using the strategies that they have learnt.
Remind the children to check their answers by asking: *Does it look right? Does it sound right? Does it make sense in the sentence?*
Avoid over-emphasising the spelling of each word as you read it.

>   Read each word aloud, saying: *The word is…*
>   Next, read the sentence that includes the word.
>   Wait for the children to attempt to write the word.
>   Re-read the word, saying: *The word is…*

Remind the children to check the word before moving to the next spelling.
At the end of the test, read each sentence again and encourage the children to check back.

Instructions for children

(You may like to read this to the children prior to the test.)

This is a spelling test to check your knowledge of the spelling patterns we have worked on this half term.
You need a pencil.
Please write your name, class and the date at the top of the test.
I will read a word out loud and then say it again in a sentence.
You should write the word in the gap in the sentence on your test.
I will read it again and give you time to check it.
Don't worry if you are not sure about a spelling. Have a go using the strategies we have learnt.
If you make a mistake, cross out the word and try again.

Words tested (20)

farther, passed, steal, effect, complement, heard, principal, who's, ascent, desert, led, profit, aisle, bridal, draft, morning, stationary, aloud, cereal, weigh

Year 5/P6 Summer Half Term 2 Test A

Spelling script

Spelling 1: The word is **farther**.
The beach was **farther** away than we thought.
The word is **farther**.

Spelling 2: The word is **passed**.
I saw the big wheel as we **passed** the fairground.
The word is **passed**.

Spelling 3: The word is **steal**.
The children plotted to **steal** the chocolate biscuits.
The word is **steal**.

Spelling 4: The word is **effect**.
The hay fever medicine had no **effect** at all on the sneezing girl.
The word is **effect**.

Spelling 5: The word is **complement**.
The sauce was a perfect **complement** to the pudding.
The word is **complement**.

Spelling 6: The word is **heard**.
The teacher **heard** the girls across the playground.
The word is **heard**.

Spelling 7: The word is **principal**.
The **principal** reason for exercising is to keep your body healthy.
The word is **principal**.

Spelling 8: The word is **who's** (the contraction of *who is*).
Who's coming to the park after school?
The word is **who's**.

Spelling 9: The word is **ascent**.
We made the final **ascent** to the top of the mountain.
The word is **ascent**.

Spelling 10: The word is **desert**.
Camels are known as the ships of the **desert**.
The word is **desert**.

Spelling 11: The word is **led**.
We **led** the horses into their grazing field.
The word is **led**.

Spelling 12: The word is **profit**.
The entrepreneurs aimed to make a healthy **profit**.
The word is **profit**.

Spelling 13: The word is **aisle**.
The bride glided down the **aisle** of the church.
The word is **aisle.**

Spelling 14: The word is **bridal**.
Her sister's **bridal** gown was made from ivory satin.
The word is **bridal**.

Spelling 15: The word is **draft**.
The first **draft** of the report needed some work to improve it.
The word is **draft**.

Spelling 16: The word is **morning**.
We awoke early in the **morning** to go for a swim.
The word is **morning**.

Spelling 17: The word is **stationary**.
We boarded the **stationary** fairground ride and prepared for the thrill of our lives.
The word is **stationary**.

Spelling 18: The word is **aloud**.
Please read **aloud** the statement.
The word is **aloud**.

Spelling 19: The word is **cereal**.
The **cereal** bowl spilled over with crunchy wheat flakes.
The word is **cereal**.

Spelling 20: The word is **weigh**.
The vet needed to **weigh** the kitten each week to check its growth.
The word is **weigh**.

Well done! Now I will read the sentences again so you can check your spelling.

Year 5/P6 Summer Half Term 2 Test A

1. The beach was _____ away than we thought.

2. I saw the big wheel as we _____ the fairground.

3. The children plotted to _____ the chocolate biscuits.

4. The hay fever medicine had no _____ at all on the

    sneezing girl.

5. The sauce was a perfect _____ to the pudding.

6. The teacher _____ the girls across the playground.

7. The _____ reason for exercising is to keep your body

    healthy.

8. _____ coming to the park after school?

9. We made the final _____ to the top of the mountain.

10. Camels are known as the ships of the _____.

11. We _____ the horses into their grazing field.

12. The entrepreneurs aimed to make a healthy _____.

13. The bride glided down the _____ of the church.

14. Her sister's _____ gown was made from ivory satin.

15. The first _____ of the report needed some work to

improve it.

16. We awoke early in the _____ to go for a swim.

17. We boarded the _____ fairground ride and prepared for

the thrill of our lives.

18. Please read _____ the statement.

19. The _____ bowl spilled over with crunchy wheat flakes.

20. The vet needed to _____ the kitten each week to check

its growth.

Total _____ / 20

Year 5/P6 Summer Half Term 2 Test B

Spelling rules and knowledge

- Homophones and other easily confused words

Guidance for teachers

The test is designed to build experience and confidence with this format, as well as to test children's spelling knowledge.

The test should take approximately 15 minutes.

Children should have a copy of the test and a pencil to use.

Children with specific needs should be given appropriate support.

All children should be encouraged to have a go at spelling each word, using the strategies that they have learnt.

Remind the children to check their answers by asking: *Does it look right? Does it sound right? Does it make sense in the sentence?*

Avoid over-emphasising the spelling of each word as you read it.

Read each word aloud, saying: *The word is…*
Next, read the sentence that includes the word.
Wait for the children to attempt to write the word.
Re-read the word, saying: *The word is…*

Remind the children to check the word before moving to the next spelling.

At the end of the test, read each sentence again and encourage the children to check back.

Instructions for children

(You may like to read this to the children prior to the test.)

This is a spelling test to check your knowledge of the spelling patterns we have worked on this half term.

You need a pencil.

Please write your name, class and the date at the top of the test.

I will read a word out loud and then say it again in a sentence.

You should write the word in the gap in the sentence on your test.

I will read it again and give you time to check it.

Don't worry if you are not sure about a spelling. Have a go using the strategies we have learnt.

If you make a mistake, cross out the word and try again.

Words tested (20)

guessed, proceed, wary, alter, descent, father, past, steel, affect, compliment, lead, prophet, isle, bridle, draught, mourning, stationery, allowed, serial, way

Year 5/P6 Summer Half Term 2 Test B

Spelling script

Spelling 1: The word is **guessed**.
Nobody **guessed** the identity of the masked
highwayman.
The word is **guessed**.

Spelling 2: The word is **proceed**.
We were asked to **proceed** towards the exit.
The word is **proceed**.

Spelling 3: The word is **wary**.
The kitten was **wary** of Grandad's furry slippers.
The word is **wary**.

Spelling 4: The word is **alter**.
He was messy and could not **alter** his behaviour.
The word is **alter**.

Spelling 5: The word is **descent**.
The **descent** into town took just two minutes on skis!
The word is **descent**.

Spelling 6: The word is **father**.
Their **father** dived into the swimming pool and made
an enormous splash.
The word is **father**.

Spelling 7: The word is **past**.
In the **past**, we had fewer machines to help in the
home.
The word is **past**.

Spelling 8: The word is **steel**.
The **steel** bike was heavier than the carbon frame.
The word is **steel**.

Spelling 9: The word is **affect**.
How did the sad movie **affect** you?
The word is **affect**.

Spelling 10: The word is **compliment**.
He struggled to give her a **compliment**, despite
admiring her photographs.
The word is **compliment**.

Spelling 11: The word is **lead**.
Some water pipes used to be made from **lead**, but
now we know it can be dangerous.
The word is **lead**.

Spelling 12: The word is **prophet**.
A **prophet** is someone who predicts the future.
The word is **prophet**.

Spelling 13: The word is **isle**.
An **isle** is a small island, and several can be found
off the coast of the UK.
The word is **isle**.

Spelling 14: The word is **bridle**.
The horse's **bridle** was too tight.
The word is **bridle**.

Spelling 15: The word is **draught**.
There was a **draught** blowing through the tent.
The word is **draught**.

Spelling 16: The word is **mourning**.
People in **mourning** often where black.
The word is **mourning**.

Spelling 17: The word is **stationery**.
She loved to buy new **stationery** every year.
The word is **stationery**.

Spelling 18: The word is **allowed**.
The children were not **allowed** to play on their
mobile phones in the car.
The word is **allowed**.

Spelling 19: The word is **serial**.
Their feisty cat was a **serial** wildlife killer!
The word is **serial**.

Spelling 20: The word is **way**.
She went out of her **way** to make a splendid birthday
cake for her daughter.
The word is **way**.

Well done! Now I will read the sentences again so you can check your spelling.

Name   Class   Date

Year 5/P6 Summer Half Term 2 Test B

1. Nobody _____ the identity of the masked highwayman.

2. We were asked to _____ towards the exit.

3. The kitten was _____ of Grandad's furry slippers.

4. He was messy and could not _____ his behaviour.

5. The _____ into town took just two minutes on skis!

6. Their _____ dived into the swimming pool and made an

   enormous splash.

7. In the _____, we had fewer machines to help in the home.

8. The _____ bike was heavier than the carbon frame.

9. How did the sad movie _____ you?

10. He struggled to give her a _____, despite admiring her

    photographs.

11. Some water pipes used to be made from _____, but now we

    know it can be dangerous.

12. A _____ is someone who predicts the future.

13. An _____ is a small island, and several can be found off the

    coast of the UK.

14. The horse's _____ was too tight.

15. There was a _____ blowing through the tent.

16. People in _____ often wear black.

17. She loved to buy new _____ every year.

18. The children were not _____ to play on their mobile phones

    in the car.

19. Their feisty cat was a _____ wildlife killer!

20. She went out of her _____ to make a splendid birthday cake

    for her daughter.

Total _____ / 20

Answers in Context

Year 5/P6 Autumn Half Term 1 Test A

1. The crown was dotted with **precious** sapphires.

2. The **cautious** vet edged nearer to the injured dog.

3. For a **special** treat, we stayed up until midnight.

4. The **confidential** document was left on the seat of the train.

5. The **expectant** children couldn't wait for the day of the party.

6. The **delicious** cake attracted the girl's attention.

7. The deadly virus was terribly **infectious**.

8. The bank manager dealt with the **financial** matters.

9. The **initial** letter is used to arrange words in alphabetical order.

10. The **tolerant** Labrador allowed the children to pull its ears.

Answers in Context

11. She was **anxious** when her brother didn't arrive home at the usual time.

12. The **pretentious** footballer thought he should play for the Premier League.

13. It is **crucial** to wear a seatbelt in a car.

14. The children couldn't wait for their **residential** trip.

15. The shop **assistant** brought me some jeans to try.

16. The boy's new bedroom was extremely **spacious**.

17. A **scrumptious** feast awaited the guests.

18. The **official** letter arrived in a brown envelope marked 'confidential'.

19. We spend a **substantial** amount of time outside in the garden.

20. We could see the sun rising on the **distant** horizon.

Answers in Context

Year 5/P6 Autumn Half Term 1 Test B

1. The **vicious** dog snarled at the quivering thief.

2. In an **ambitious** move, the defender slid to the left.

3. The royal wedding was the **social** event of the year.

4. Ferns prefer to grow in **partial** shade.

5. A detective needs to be **observant** to spot clues.

6. Although he banged his head on the pavement, he remained **conscious**.

7. Traditional stories like Little Red Riding Hood are **fictitious**, rather than true.

8. Robots can use **artificial** intelligence to build cars.

9. It is **essential** to brush your teeth at least twice a day!

10. She became **hesitant** when she saw the height of the diving board.

Answers in Context

11. The **malicious** bully sneered at the trembling child.

12. Lentils are highly **nutritious**.

13. The television **commercial** for fast food was banned from children's TV.

14. We stayed in luxury at the **palatial** holiday home.

15. The police officer only wanted to record **relevant** facts about the incident.

16. My brother's smiling face made me **suspicious**.

17. A **conscientious** child does their homework without being asked.

18. The country town had a **provincial** look about it.

19. Sports people aim to fulfil their **potential**.

20. He was **reluctant** to spend too much money on new trainers.

Answers in Context

Year 5/P6 Autumn Half Term 2 Test A

1. Would you like **assistance** with your suitcase?

2. The lifeboat's **buoyancy** was reducing by the second.

3. You made a **decent** attempt at tidying up.

4. The teenager was desperate to be given more **independence**.

5. We can speak French with **fluency**.

6. Sugar on strawberries is a delicious **extravagance**.

7. His feeling of **complacency** was destroyed when he lost the game.

8. We are **confident** about our spelling ability!

9. The detective scoured the garden for **evidence** of the crime.

10. There is absolutely no **urgency** to get out of bed.

Answers in Context

11. The teacher's **tolerance** was tested by the flickering lights!

12. **Truancy** is a problem in some secondary schools.

13. I tried on **different** trainers, but they still pinched my toes.

14. The **silence** was rather unnerving.

15. In an **emergency**, please leave by the nearest exit.

16. They showed **resistance** by refusing to wear the new uniform.

17. The **stagnancy** of the water made it undrinkable.

18. The man's tattoo was a **permanent** reminder of his love for his wife.

19. Some say that **patience** is a virtue!

20. A **deficiency** in vitamins can make you feel unwell.

Answers in Context

Year 5/P6 Autumn Half Term 2 Test B

1. There was an **abundance** of apples in the orchard.

2. There was **hesitancy** in her voice as she sang.

3. The **innocent** girl was wrongly accused of stealing.

4. Our puppy goes to **obedience** classes.

5. The dress **agency** sells ball gowns and tiaras.

6. His **dominance** on the field was obvious when he scored a try.

7. There was a **discrepancy** between what he earned and what he was paid.

8. On **frequent** occasions she got distracted.

9. The storyteller's **presence** filled them with suspense.

10. Her **decency** showed when she donated her gift to the charity.

Answers in Context

11. Mum loves to wear French **fragrance**.

12. In early **infancy**, some children go to pre-school.

13. I feel **independent** when I ride my bike.

14. The judge gave a harsh **sentence** to the car thief.

15. She had a **tendency** to speak without thinking.

16. His **ignorance** of the school rules led him into trouble.

17. The man used his **redundancy** pay to buy a new caravan.

18. We try not to be **absent** from school on too many occasions.

19. A strange **sequence** of events led to his disappearance.

20. I try to eat green vegetables with increased **frequency**.

Answers in Context

Year 5/P6 Spring Half Term 1 Test A

1. There was **considerable** tension in the exam room.

2. Her excitement about the new bike was **understandable**.

3. The burnt toast was barely **edible**.

4. Despite the argument, they left the playground **amicably**.

5. It was **terribly** hot in the greenhouse.

6. The weather in the morning is forecast to be **changeable**.

7. The trip to the cinema was really **enjoyable**.

8. His **incredible** memory allowed him to learn whole poems with ease.

9. He failed **miserably** when he tried to cheer her up.

10. The test seemed **impossibly** difficult.

Answers in Context

11.   The scar on his cheek was barely **noticeable**.

12.   He was a **reliable** helper who never failed to turn up.

13.   The music from his headphones was **audible** from the other side

of the room.

14.   She behaved **honourably**, despite her desire to make a fuss.

15.   **Sensibly**, the children lined up at the door.

16.   The boy learnt a **valuable** lesson when he listened to the story.

17.   The tap water in the hostel was **drinkable**.

18.   Is it **possible** to ride a bike safely with no hands?

19.   The temperature in the room became **noticeably** cooler.

20.   Some bears are **irresistibly** attracted to honey.

Answers in Context

Year 5/P6 Spring Half Term 1 Test B

1. The **adorable** kitten attracted the girls' attention.

2. She was the most **dependable** volunteer and always wanted to help.

3. The guards made a **forcible** entry into the prisoner's cell.

4. She turned up **reliably**, time after time.

5. It was **possibly** the wettest day of the whole summer.

6. His prickly heat rash was barely **tolerable**.

7. The new computer game was a **reasonable** price.

8. The skier was barely **visible** on the snowy hillside.

9. The little children queued **excitably** for the bouncy castle.

10. She was **visibly** upset by the sad story.

Answers in Context

11. The **sociable** bus driver greeted all his passengers with "Hello!"

12. The butter was so cold that it was barely **mixable**.

13. You have just made a very **sensible** suggestion.

14. She was **laughably** late for the interview.

15. She crept **invisibly** into the back of the cave and hid from the hunter.

16. Your footwear isn't **suitable** for the muddy park.

17. The writing on the treasure map was barely **readable**.

18. The gymnast's body was strong and **flexible**.

19. I am **reasonably** confident that we will win the cup.

20. He walked the dog **responsibly** along the busy road.

Answers in Context

Year 5/P6 Spring Half Term 2 Test A

1.   She **referred** to the dictionary to check the spelling.

2.   They could not be **deterred** from eating the cake!

3.   When you **co-operate**, you can achieve more than on your own.

4.   He was ready to **receive** his medal from the judge.

5.   The teacher wanted his children to **achieve** the best results possible.

6.   The **reference** book fell open at the picture of the huge tarantula.

7.   We can **transfer** the co-ordinates to the map.

8.   The girls were prepared to **co-own** the pony.

9.   The **ceiling** needed painting following the fizzy drink explosion.

10.   You can make a **brief** visit to the shop today.

Answers in Context

11. The **referee** blew his whistle to end the game.

12. We struggled when **transferring** the goldfish from the jar to the fish tank.

13. It was hard to **re-orientate** ourselves when we came out into the light.

14. Meat and cheese give us **protein** in our diet.

15. Who would like a **piece** of fruit cake?

16. Please tick the menu to show your **preference**.

17. She kindly **offered** me a lift when it was raining.

18. We tried, unsuccessfully, to **re-attach** the broken handle.

19. Some fizzy drinks contain **caffeine** and food colourings.

20. His best **friend** was invited for a sleepover.

Answers in Context

Year 5/P6 Spring Half Term 2 Test B

1. He kept **referring** to his beloved pet chameleon.

2. There was no **deterring** them from their quest to reach the fifth level of the game.

3. We needed to **co-ordinate** our plans for the trip.

4. The boy's story didn't **deceive** his father.

5. She was puffed up with **conceit** at her cleverness.

6. The doctor made a **referral** for the boy to see the orthopaedic surgeon about his broken wrist.

7. Many believe that powerful weapons are no **deterrence** in a war situation.

8. We **re-use** our water bottles to help the environment.

9. Mum can **perceive** how I feel by looking at my face.

10. If you **believe** in yourself, you can succeed.

Answers in Context

11. We ran into the sea, **preferring** not to linger on the sharp pebbles.

12. The international football player was **transferred** by his club to another team.

13. Two or more children can **co-author** a story.

14. We attempted to **seize** the escaping hamster.

15. The child's tears of **grief** were wiped away by his father.

16. She **preferred** salted caramel to vanilla ice cream.

17. Thank you for **offering** to carry my heavy bag.

18. The enemies could not **co-exist** in the same room.

19. He had **neither** the will nor the desire to join in with the game of volleyball.

20. It was such a **relief** to finish the marathon!

Answers in Context

Year 5/P6 Summer Half Term 1 Test A

1. We **bought** a new game for our console.

2. **Although** it was really late, we pleaded to stay up until the end of the film.

3. Can you swim to the **island** and back before tea?

4. She tried to **comb** her tangled hair without crying.

5. He tried to **advise** his son on which skills he should develop on the pitch.

6. We **brought** our PE kit to school for sports day.

7. The child made a **thorough** search of the playground.

8. The **thistle** became tangled in the dog's fur.

9. Every **muscle** in their bodies ached after the hike.

10. Dad needed to get a fishing **licence** for our day at the river.

Answers in Context

11. He put special tyres on his mountain bike to cope with the **rough** ground.

12. The farmer had to **plough** the field before planting.

13. She repaid her **debt**, one pound at a time.

14. My **knee** was bruised when I fell off my skateboard.

15. The **practice** was open for patients every morning at 8:00 a.m.

16. You need to drink **enough** water to keep you well-hydrated on a hot day.

17. The **borough** council planted more trees.

18. Sometimes a **hymn** is sung at a church wedding.

19. The little boy sucked his **thumb** for comfort.

20. The children tried to **devise** a plan to avoid doing their homework.

Answers in Context

Year 5/P6 Summer Half Term 1 Test B

1. We **thought** that the referee's decision was fair.

2. We make bread **dough** using wholemeal flour.

3. The **lamb** was given a blue mark to identify it.

4. To be a good drummer requires a strong sense of **rhythm**.

5. Please turn off your mobile **device**!

6. You **ought** to be in bed by now.

7. Even **though** it was raining, the children wanted to bounce on the trampoline.

8. She did not **doubt** his story about the lost homework.

9. The **castle** was stormed by armoured soldiers.

10. Mum sought **advice** from a gardening expert before choosing new plants.

Answers in Context

11. The marathon runners had to be **tough** to finish the race.

12. The children nestled in the **bough** of the tree.

13. The old stone **tomb** was deathly cold and covered in moss.

14. The vet wrapped a bandage around the dog's damaged **limb**.

15. You need to **practise** the piano every day.

16. His hacking **cough** kept him awake at night.

17. The farmer filled the **trough** with hay for the ponies.

18. We dared him to **knock** on the solid oak door.

19. Do you **know** how to mend a puncture?

20. The council agreed to **license** the building for the party.

Answers in Context

Year 5/P6 Summer Half Term 2 Test A

1. The beach was **farther** away than we thought.

2. I saw the big wheel as we **passed** the fairground.

3. The children plotted to **steal** the chocolate biscuits.

4. The hay fever medicine had no **effect** at all on the sneezing girl.

5. The sauce was a perfect **complement** to the pudding.

6. The teacher **heard** the girls across the playground.

7. The **principal** reason for exercising is to keep your body healthy.

8. **Who's** coming to the park after school?

9. We made the final **ascent** to the top of the mountain.

10. Camels are known as the ships of the **desert**.

Answers in Context

11. We **led** the horses into their grazing field.

12. The entrepreneurs aimed to make a healthy **profit**.

13. The bride glided down the **aisle** of the church.

14. Her sister's **bridal** gown was made from ivory satin.

15. The first **draft** of the report needed some work to improve it.

16. We awoke early in the **morning** to go for a swim.

17. We boarded the **stationary** fairground ride and prepared for the thrill of our lives.

18. Please read **aloud** the statement.

19. The **cereal** bowl spilled over with crunchy wheat flakes.

20. The vet needed to **weigh** the kitten each week to check its growth.

Answers in Context

Year 5/P6 Summer Half Term 2 Test B

1. Nobody **guessed** the identity of the masked highwayman.

2. We were asked to **proceed** towards the exit.

3. The kitten was **wary** of Grandad's furry slippers.

4. He was messy and could not **alter** his behaviour.

5. The **descent** into town took just two minutes on skis!

6. Their **father** dived into the swimming pool and made an enormous splash.

7. In the **past**, we had fewer machines to help in the home.

8. The **steel** bike was heavier than the carbon frame.

9. How did the sad movie **affect** you?

10. He struggled to give her a **compliment**, despite admiring her photographs.

Answers in Context

11. Some water pipes used to be made from **lead**, but now we know it can be dangerous.

12. A **prophet** is someone who predicts the future.

13. An **isle** is a small island, and several can be found off the coast of the UK.

14. The horse's **bridle** was too tight.

15. There was a **draught** blowing through the tent.

16. People in **mourning** often wear black.

17. She loved to buy new **stationery** every year.

18. The children were not **allowed** to play on their mobile phones in the car.

19. Their feisty cat was a **serial** wildlife killer!

20. She went out of her **way** to make a splendid birthday cake for her daughter.

Word-only Answers

Year 5/P6 Autumn Half Term 1 Test A

1. precious, 2. cautious, 3. special,
4. confidential, 5. expectant, 6. delicious,
7. infectious, 8. financial, 9. initial, 10. tolerant,
11. anxious, 12. pretentious, 13. crucial,
14. residential, 15. assistant, 16. spacious,
17. scrumptious, 18. official, 19. substantial,
20. distant

Year 5/P6 Autumn Half Term 1 Test B

1. vicious, 2. ambitious, 3. social, 4. partial,
5. observant, 6. conscious, 7. fictitious,
8. artificial, 9. essential, 10. hesitant,
11. malicious, 12. nutritious, 13. commercial,
14. palatial, 15. relevant, 16. suspicious,
17. conscientious, 18. provincial, 19. potential,
20. reluctant

Year 5/P6 Autumn Half Term 2 Test A

1. assistance, 2. buoyancy, 3. decent,
4. independence, 5. fluency, 6. extravagance,
7. complacency, 8. confident, 9. evidence,
10. urgency, 11. tolerance, 12. truancy,
13. different, 14. silence, 15. emergency,
16. resistance, 17. stagnancy, 18. permanent,
19. patience, 20. deficiency

Year 5/P6 Autumn Half Term 2 Test B

1. abundance, 2. hesitancy, 3. innocent,
4. obedience, 5. agency, 6. dominance,
7. discrepancy, 8. frequent, 9. presence,
10. decency, 11. fragrance, 12. infancy,
13. independent, 14. sentence, 15. tendency,
16. ignorance, 17. redundancy, 18. absent,
19. sequence, 20. frequency

Year 5/P6 Spring Half Term 1 Test A

1. considerable, 2. understandable, 3. edible,
4. amicably, 5. terribly, 6. changeable,
7. enjoyable, 8. incredible, 9. miserably,
10. impossibly, 11. noticeable, 12. reliable,
13. audible, 14. honourably, 15. sensibly,
16. valuable, 17. drinkable, 18. possible,
19. noticeably, 20. irresistibly

Year 5/P6 Spring Half Term 1 Test B

1. adorable, 2. dependable, 3. forcible,
4. reliably, 5. possibly, 6. tolerable,
7. reasonable, 8. visible, 9. excitably, 10.
visibly, 11. sociable, 12. mixable, 13. sensible,
14. laughably, 15. invisibly, 16. suitable,
17. readable, 18. flexible, 19. reasonably,
20. responsibly

Year 5/P6 Spring Half Term 2 Test A

1. referred, 2. deterred, 3. co-operate, 4.
receive, 5. achieve, 6. reference, 7. transfer, 8.
co-own,
9. ceiling, 10. brief, 11. referee, 12. transferring,
13. re-orientate, 14. protein, 15. piece,
16. preference, 17. offered, 18. re-attach,
19. caffeine, 20. friend

Year 5/P6 Spring Half Term 2 Test B

1. referring, 2. deterring, 3. co-ordinate,
4. deceive, 5. conceit, 6. referral, 7. deterrence,
8. re-use, 9. perceive, 10. believe, 11.
preferring, 12. transferred, 13. co-author, 14.
seize,
15. grief, 16. preferred, 17. offering, 18. co-
exist, 19. neither, 20. relief

Word-only Answers

Year 5/P6 Summer Half Term 1 Test A
1. bought, 2. although, 3. island, 4. comb,
5. advise, 6. brought, 7. thorough, 8. thistle,
9. muscle, 10. licence, 11. rough, 12. plough,
13. debt, 14. knee, 15. practice, 16. enough,
17. borough, 18. hymn, 19. thumb, 20. devise

Year 5/P6 Summer Half Term 1 Test B
1. thought, 2. dough, 3. lamb, 4. rhythm,
5. device, 6. ought, 7. though, 8. doubt, 9.
castle, 10. advice, 11. tough, 12. bough, 13.
tomb,
14. limb, 15. practise, 16. cough, 17. trough,
18. knock, 19. know, 20. license

Year 5/P6 Summer Half Term 2 Test A
1. farther, 2. passed, 3. steal, 4. effect,
5. complement, 6. heard, 7. principal, 8. who's,
9. ascent, 10. desert, 11. led, 12. profit, 13.
aisle, 14. bridal, 15. draft, 16. morning, 17.
stationary, 18. aloud, 19. cereal, 20. weigh

Year 5/P6 Summer Half Term 2 Test B
1. guessed, 2. proceed, 3. wary, 4. alter,
5. descent, 6. father, 7. past, 8. steel, 9. affect,
10. compliment, 11. lead, 12. prophet, 13. isle,
14. bridle, 15. draught, 16. mourning,
17. stationery, 18. allowed, 19. serial, 20. way

Name			Class

Year 5/P6 Spelling Record Sheet

Tests	Mark	Total marks	Key words to target
Autumn Half Term 1 Test A		20	
Autumn Half Term 1 Test B		20	
Autumn Half Term 2 Test A		20	
Autumn Half Term 2 Test B		20	
Spring Half Term 1 Test A		20	
Spring Half Term 1 Test B		20	
Spring Half Term 2 Test A		20	
Spring Half Term 2 Test B		20	
Summer Half Term 1 Test A		20	
Summer Half Term 1 Test B		20	
Summer Half Term 2 Test A		20	
Summer Half Term 2 Test B		20